GREAT CAREERS IN
TECHNOLOGY

by Connor Stratton

FOCUS
READERS.

NAVIGATOR

WWW.FOCUSREADERS.COM

Focus Readers is distributed by North Star Editions:
sales@northstareditions.com | 888-417-0195

Produced for Focus Readers by Red Line Editorial.

Photographs ©: Shutterstock Images, cover, 1, 4–5, 7, 8–9, 11, 13, 15, 16–17, 19, 21, 22–23, 25, 26–27; Red Line Editorial, 29

Library of Congress Cataloging-in-Publication Data
Names: Stratton, Connor, author.
Title: Great careers in technology / by Connor Stratton.
Description: Lake Elmo, MN : Focus Readers, [2022] | Includes index. | Audience: Grades 4-6.
Identifiers: LCCN 2021011883 (print) | LCCN 2021011884 (ebook) | ISBN 9781644938492 (hardcover) | ISBN 9781644938959 (paperback) | ISBN 9781644939833 (ebook pdf) | ISBN 9781644939413 (hosted ebook)
Subjects: LCSH: Computer science--Vocational guidance--Juvenile literature. | Information technology--Vocational guidance--Juvenile literature.
Classification: LCC QA76.23 .S77 2022 (print) | LCC QA76.23 (ebook) | DDC 004.023--dc23
LC record available at https://lccn.loc.gov/2021011883
LC ebook record available at https://lccn.loc.gov/2021011884

Printed in the United States of America
Mankato, MN
082021

ABOUT THE AUTHOR

Connor Stratton writes and edits nonfiction children's books. His family first got a computer in the late 1990s. It held a whopping 1.96 gigabytes of storage space.

TABLE OF CONTENTS

CHAPTER 1

WORKING IN TECHNOLOGY

When people think of careers in technology, they often imagine **programmers** writing code. However, programming is just one of the many careers in technology. Web developers build websites. They keep sites running well, too. Computer support specialists work directly with users. They help people

Experts believe more than 500,000 technology jobs will be created between 2019 and 2029.

solve computer problems. Other careers in technology are less visible.

Companies often handle huge amounts of information. To do so, they use computer **networks**. Network architects help design those networks. Companies also use computer systems. Analysts work to improve those systems. Then **administrators** make sure everything runs smoothly. Some administrators manage **databases**. Others manage networks. Finally, many people work in information security. They help protect companies' data.

Computers are complex. They involve many parts. **Hardware** workers create the

Network administrators make sure a company's computers can communicate with one another.

physical parts of computers. In addition, computer scientists study new ways to use technology.

CHAPTER 2

DEVELOPERS AND PROGRAMMERS

Developers and programmers are two of the most common careers in technology. Developers are similar to architects. But instead of designing buildings, they design **software**. Some developers work on programs for desktop computers. Others work on applications for phones and tablets. Developers try to

Developers must consider how users will experience their programs and apps.

design apps that are easy and satisfying to use.

Developers send their designs to computer programmers. If developers are like architects, then programmers are like construction workers. Programmers

WHAT IS CODE?

Code tells computers what to do. It is a series of step-by-step instructions. Computers understand one kind of code. It is known as machine language. But machine language is made up of 1s and 0s. It's hard for people to write code that way. So, people developed many other programming languages. These languages are easier for people to understand. Later, they get turned into machine language for the computer.

Errors are more likely to happen if code is complex. So, programmers often look for ways to make code simpler.

actually create the apps. To do so, they write code. Code controls how each part of an app will work.

Programmers also change existing code. Programs and apps need to be updated often. For example, users might find a problem with a program. Or an app might need to work with a new kind of phone. When those things happen, programmers update the code.

Sometimes, developers do their own programming. In smaller companies, one person often performs both roles. These workers design programs. Then they write code to create those programs.

Web development is also a common career in technology. Web developers focus on websites. Front-end web developers deal with the sites that users see. They make websites user-friendly. Back-end developers make sure the sites run smoothly. This job might involve many tasks. For example, online stores must have payment options. Back-end developers make sure payment processes work. Users do not see this kind of work. But without it, sites would not function.

FRONT-END VS. BACK-END

FRONT-END TASKS

- MAKE SURE WEBSITE IS USER-FRIENDLY
- MAKE SURE WEBSITE WORKS ON DIFFERENT BROWSERS
- USE LANGUAGES SUCH AS HTML, CSS, AND JAVASCRIPT

BACK-END TASKS

- MAKE SURE WEBSITE IS FAST AND SECURE
- DEAL WITH DATA STORAGE
- USE PROGRAMMING LANGUAGES SUCH AS PYTHON, RUBY, AND PERL

GAME DEVELOPERS

Video games often feature stories, characters, and worlds. Many people work together to bring games to life. Writers come up with stories and goals. Artists illustrate characters and worlds. Designers work with all these ideas. Then they explain the ideas to game developers.

Game developers are programmers. They use code. This code makes the games' ideas happen. For example, some games try to be realistic. That's when actions look like they do in the real world. When characters jump, they fall back to the ground. Other games are not like the real world. Characters can fly or breathe fire.

Either way, code makes the rules for games. It tells computers how to respond. Getting the code

Quality assurance testers make sure video games work as intended.

right can be a lot of work. So, people often use game engines to help. These software tools help handle the details of each game.

CHAPTER 3

NETWORKS AND SYSTEMS

Many skilled workers help companies manage their data. Network architects design networks for storing and sharing information. For example, an office might use a local area network (LAN). LANs connect computers in a small area, such as a building. LANs let those computers share information.

Network architects are some of the highest-paid people in technology.

However, a company might have offices in several cities. LANs would not work in this case. So, network architects may use **cloud** technology. Cloud networks use the internet to handle information. These networks can connect computers in different areas.

CLOUDS ON THE GROUND

Around the world, data centers store people's cloud data. Some centers are massive. Nevada is home to a data center that covers 1.3 million square feet (121,000 sq m). That's the size of 22 football fields. Many employees keep data centers running. The centers are staffed 24 hours a day. Workers make sure the cloud never goes down.

Large data centers have row upon row of high-powered computers.

Companies also hire systems analysts. These workers study the computer systems that companies use. They find new programs and applications. Then they help companies use those technologies. Systems analysts also try to make computer systems more **efficient**. That way, companies save money.

Administrators run these technologies day-to-day. Network administrators make sure the networks run smoothly. They fix problems as they come up. In addition, they handle network updates. Systems administrators help **install** new programs. They fix system errors. They often manage company hardware, too. Database administrators manage a company's information. They organize data. They also help employees access it.

Information security is another important field. Many companies collect personal data. For example, banks have people's financial information. Banks must keep that data private. That way,

An information security worker may help hospitals keep patients' health records private.

people do not have their money stolen. Information security workers protect companies' data. They maintain security systems. And they help prevent **hacks**. They also find the least-secure parts of a system. Then workers come up with ways to increase security.

CHAPTER 4

PEOPLE, PARTS, AND IDEAS

Technology is not always easy to use. People might need help learning how to use a new app. Or a computer might stop working. That's where support specialists come in. Support specialists work directly with users. They help people figure out solutions to technology problems.

Support specialists may speak to users on the phone to help them deal with computer problems.

Sometimes the software is not the problem. The technology might need new hardware. Computers are made of many parts. Hardware technicians replace computer parts. They repair parts, too. Hardware engineers design new parts. They try to build better hardware.

ARTIFICIAL INTELLIGENCE

Computer scientists often develop the newest fields of technology. One major field is artificial intelligence (AI). Some AI can recognize people's faces. Other AI helps doctors find diseases. Computer scientists also build AI robots. Some of these robots can understand emotions on human faces. Scientists even teach computers to write poetry. The possibilities of AI technology are vast.

The central processing unit is like a computer's brain. It processes the user's commands, such as pressing a key.

Sometimes the technology to solve a problem doesn't exist yet. But a computer scientist might be working on it. Computer scientists develop new ideas about technology. Some create new coding languages. Others run computer experiments. Computer scientists help shape the future of technology.

CHAPTER 5

ENTERING THE FIELD

Technology careers vary widely. Some jobs require a two-year associate's degree. These jobs include support specialists and web developers. However, most technology careers require a four-year bachelor's degree. These jobs include software developers and computer programmers. Many technology

Taking coding classes is a great way to prepare for a career in technology.

workers study computer science in college.

Some careers require more education after college. For example, computer scientists get advanced degrees in the field. Systems analysts may go to business school. In addition, workers often learn about related fields. Technology jobs are everywhere. They play roles in health care, finance, and government. So, workers learn how technology can improve those fields.

Certain skills are helpful for most technology careers. People often need some knowledge of code. They also need to solve complex problems. Critical thinking is important. Paying attention to details matters, too. Technology work can also be very creative. People must think of new solutions. Working in technology is exciting and rewarding.

CAREER PREP CHECKLIST

Interested in a career in technology? As you move into middle school and high school, try these steps.

1. Study hard in school. Take classes in computer science and math.

2. Learn to code. Start with basic languages, such as HTML, CSS, and Java. Take coding classes in person or online.

3. Tell a guidance counselor about your interest. This person can help you find opportunities to get experience in computer science.

4. See if your area has summer camps or after-school programs in computer science and technology. Use the internet to find these opportunities.

5. Research the newest ideas related to technology.

6. Research what people who work in technology are currently doing or exploring. Ask a librarian for help finding books and websites where you can learn more.

FOCUS ON
GREAT CAREERS IN TECHNOLOGY

Write your answers on a separate piece of paper.

1. Write a paragraph explaining the main ideas of Chapter 2.

2. Do you think being a software developer or a computer programmer would be more interesting? Why?

3. What kind of web developer focuses on the part of websites that users see?

    A. front-end
    B. back-end
    C. network

4. Why might a network architect use cloud computing for a company with many offices?

    A. Cloud computing only connects computers in a small area.
    B. Cloud computing doesn't need to store any data.
    C. Cloud computing lets computers that are far apart share information easily.

Answer key on page 32.

GLOSSARY

administrators
People who manage systems or processes at work.

cloud
A system of making large amounts of computer data available through the internet.

databases
Systems that use computers to store and organize large amounts of information.

efficient
Accomplishing as much as possible with as little effort or as few resources as possible.

hacks
Times when people illegally access a computer or other device, often to cause problems or steal information.

hardware
The mechanical and electronic parts that make up a device.

install
To put code onto the device that will run a program.

networks
Systems of computers and devices that are connected to one another.

programmers
People who create, add, or change the instructions in a computer program.

software
The programs that run on a computer and perform certain functions.

TO LEARN MORE

BOOKS

Omoth, Tyler. *Busting Boredom with Technology.*
  North Mankato, MN: Capstone Press, 2017.
Slingerland, Janet. *Video Game Coding.* Lake Elmo, MN:
  Focus Readers, 2019.
Smibert, Angie. *Inside Computers.* Minneapolis: Abdo
  Publishing, 2019.

NOTE TO EDUCATORS

Visit **www.focusreaders.com** to find lesson plans,
activities, links, and other resources related to this title.

INDEX

Answer Key: **1.** Answers will vary; **2.** Answers will vary; **3.** A; **4.** C